Other books published by Operation Werewolf:

The Complete Transmissions vol. I

The Complete Zines vol. I

Vakandibók

The Complete Transmissions vol. II

The Werewolf Manifesto

Book 4

THEINNERCIRCLE

:::

by

PAUL WAGGENER

OPWW #007

Copyright © 2018 Paul Waggener

Published by Operation Werewolf

Printed by CreateSpace, an Amazon.com Company

All Rights Registered By Might.

Layout by Francisco Albanese

www.OperationWerewolf.com

.:THE INNER CIRCLE:.

by

Paul Waggener

OP:.WW:.007(77)

CONTENTS

Opening Salvo 11

Training As Ritual 15

Ultimatum 21

The Hour Of Great Contempt 25

Failure Is Not Weakness 31

Aestethic 37

Progressive Overload 45

Mannaz And Mantra 51

Jera And Yantra 63

Resistance 75

Standard Bearers 83

Bhagavan and Berkano..91

Bhagavan and Berkano
Pt. II 'Becoming Bhagavan'................................99

Runes: Pathways To Mastery........................107

How To Start A Gang: A Blueprint...............119

The Inner Circle

✠Opening Salvo✠

From the beginning of Operation Werewolf, it was clear that this was not for everyone.

This exclusivity was by design.

From the look, to the message, to the way in which it was presented, my aim was true:

> *to disseminate a distilled and fiery sermon of lupine strength that would ignite a blaze within those it was intended to find.*

This has been successful in many ways, and yet at the same time, its wider reach has allowed the borders to become indistinct, and diluted. Interlopers have adopted the symbols and speech to propagate their own message, often political, or sometimes simply imitative—a cheap copy of a copy of something that was once sharp and dangerous.

The intent and direction has been dulled and polluted by thousands of pretenders, as well as apologists who try to soften the blade of our philosophy and message to make it more palatable to all. These, above all, deserve the harshest of judgements.

Operation Werewolf is not for all. It is not egalitarian. It does not recognize halfway, or nearly there. It is not a pat on the back to say "good job" for your mediocre efforts.

It is representative of the yawning abyss that exists between wolf and man, and the transformative efforts that occur there, in that darkness, that howling and terrible void of separation from the mundane.

The Great Work must never be forgotten or diluted, and within those who carry its true fire in their hearts, it hasn't. But from time to time, the tree must be shaken by the storm to be freed of dead wood. The fields must be laid to waste by the :H:ail, so that the weaker crop dies off, and only that which has strong and deep roots can survive.

This book is a collection of essays and pieces that I felt were the best of what I produced during my time on the Oregon coast, and not made available to the wider public until now. Within them are concepts and ideas that are still germinating, growing, and being put to work in the ongoing alchemy of Operation Werewolf.

It has been my honor to meet many individuals over the last several years who embody everything this order stands for, and who understand that this is a process that never ends.

While many have come to the blaze we have created and made off with scraps, skulking back into shadow with already dying embers of a flame that other men have built, lit and maintained—those loyal remain, and keep the fire burning.

They know that there is only one true cult of wolves, and they have sought it out, allied themselves with it, and added their power and glory to it.

This work is for them, and for all who breathlessly seek the center of the black sun.

✠Training as Ritual✠

According to Merriam-Webster, a ritual is

> "a sequence of activities involving gestures, words, and objects, performed in a sequestered place, and performed according to set sequence."

On that bastion of internet wisdom known as Wikipedia, the etymology of the word is described thusly:

> The English word "ritual" derives from the Latin *ritualis*, "that which pertains to rite *(ritus)*". In Roman juridical and religious usage, *ritus* was the proven way *(mos)* of doing something, or "correct performance, custom". The original

concept of *ritus* may be related to the Sanskrit *ṛtá* ("visible order)" in Vedic religion, "the lawful and regular order of the normal, and therefore proper, natural and true structure of cosmic, worldly, human and ritual events".

While reading these descriptions one morning, I was struck by the fact that they could easily be applied to lifting weights, martial arts, and other forms of physical training (and for that matter to most everything else, but I'll get to that in the next issue).

When we train, we are going to a place set aside for it, and engaging in a sequence of actions that are dictated by a proven way of doing them, whether this is for bodybuilding, powerlifting, or jiu jitsu. But more than this, we are partaking in a re-ordering of our world—an act of literal self- creation as we deliberately and consistently change not only our physical form through training, but our minds as well. There have been numerous studies done on the effect of training (both basic exercise, weightlifting and martial arts) on the human brain, and the data is definitely indicative of a positive outcome on the mind as well as the body.

We sacralize items through their use in these rituals—the favorite barbell or squat rack. The jiu jitsu gi, or boxing gloves. The embroidered weightlifting belt, and so on. This idea of making things holy, or set apart for specific use is very much in keeping with the human history of ritual and ceremony, and there is a further appeal in the sacrificial nature of training.

In his excellent article "All Training is Sacrifice," my friend and brother Jack Donovan says:

> *To train successfully, you must be willing to sacrifice portions of your present self-concept to a future, higher version of the self created by your ego. It is your ego, god-like, that is initiating and driving the process of self-transformation and becoming. This process requires you to exchange something you have for something you want. Nothing worth anything is truly free, and everything worth having requires some kind of sacrifice.*

Instead of "killing your ego" — instead of fighting yourself — approach training as a sacrifice of a part of yourself to a higher self.

This approach to training is appealing to our human need for ritual. To place our actions within a larger, mythological context in order to give our lives meaning in the grand scope of space and time—to reimagine ourselves as legendary heroes and initiates into the eternal mysteries of cosmic creation!

If we are not training as an act of ritual, why not?

If our training is informed by simple vanity, or to "look good naked," it takes on a smaller, meaner aspect, and those combined hundreds or thousands of hours spent in the gym, or in ritualized combat with other men become a massive expenditure to feed our lower ego. We will also never approach our training with the level of force and focus required to attain *Vidya*, a Sanskrit word referring to a true knowledge of something gained through direct experience of its depth.

If we are invested in the creation of our own myth through deliberate, ritual action—what kind of mythology are we creating? What does our approach to our personal rituals and ceremonies say about us as a human?

When we approach the mysteries of self-creation, it should not be with a half-hearted dedication, or with a mind that is elsewhere—thumbing through social media or texting between sets, or ignoring the cues our coach is giving us to improve our sweep or strike. If we do this, we have set ourselves up to fail, rather than to perform another critical ritual in the process of our ongoing myth.

Each rep is a prayer, every technique learned is a stepping stone, all the hours combine into a holy yes to strength, and to self improvement—to creating a legend of ourselves, and understanding on a deeper level that to train is to make ourselves like gods—that in-dwelling force representing ourselves in our absolutely highest capacity, which is the truest kind of divinity a hero can aspire toward.

"But the worst enemy you can meet will always be yourself; you lie in wait for yourself in caverns and forests. Lonely one, you are going the way to yourself! And your way goes past yourself, and past your seven devils! You will be a heretic to yourself and witch and soothsayer and fool and doubter and unholy one and villain. You must be ready to burn yourself in your own flame: how could you become new, if you had not first become ashes?"

— Friedrich Nietzsche

✠Ultimatum✠

I enjoy studying language, and the etymology of words can be a fascinating rabbit-hole, leading to a deeper grasp and more personal understanding of the sounds we use to communicate. Choosing the correct words for an idea you are trying to manifest is only as good as the understanding of those you are communicating with—this is a defining factor of the concept of mythology.

When we adopt a tribal language of symbols, words, meanings, and myth, what we are really doing is agreeing to a group definition of reality. For this reason, tribes must remain smaller expressions, tighter-knit groups who share these agreements or certain accepted truths about our existence and value system. Operation Werewolf spans continents, but within it, there is an ever-developing set of shared concepts and group-inspired verbiage and narrative. One could say that we are building our own mythology.

This mythology, as we have said in the past, is not informed by historical occurrence as much as it is by other mythological forms and constructs. Mythology is not rooted in fact, but in a truth that exists outside of space and time—it can be trusted, because it is, in a way, like a machine. Built from many small pieces, with specific purpose and goals in mind—but also rooted biologically and organically into the shadowy dawn of human existence, finding its values in those things which have remained true for many people, across many aeons or ages of this world.

One of my brothers in the Wolves said of our tribe, "it is not an organization, it is an organism." The profound nature of what he was saying applies here, too, I think. Operation Werewolf breathes and grows according to the actions and deeds of those within it who make of themselves legends—stories are told of these men and women around fires that are lit thousands of miles apart. Epic journeys are undertaken so that these men and women can meet face to face. Tattoos are applied ritually to commemorate the experience. Blood is spilled. Friendships and new brotherhoods are grown out of the soil of difficult action and long sojourn.

These experiences are there for the taking. This mythology is alive for the shaping. Will it be your actions that help it grow into a towering monolith, or will you remain silently at home? For some of you, the few who take this idea and let it grow in your hearts until it becomes an undeniable urge, I'll see you out there.

FIGVRA XCII

It is representative of the **yawning abyss** that exists between **Wolf** and **Man**, and the transformative efforts that occur there, in that **darkness**, that howling and terrible void of **separation** from the mundane.

***

+The Hour of Great Contempt+

The "logo" at the beginning of these transmissions was drawn by Ms. Sofia Buratti, of Dire Dogs Italy (some of you may be familiar with the head of the Dire Dogs, Leonardo Albiero—someone who exemplifies the Operation on many levels).

The story behind the conception of the piece came about one morning as I was walking in the pre-dawn hours down at the ocean, as has become my habit since moving to the Oregon coast. I was having one of those "what does it all mean" moments, those ones where you are trying desperately to see all the threads and pieces, and how they fit together, where you've been, where you're going, and if you're on the right track.

We all have these moments from time to time, if we are honest with ourselves and spend time in self-examination. They are sort of miniature "dark nights of the soul," where we tend to question ourselves and our decisions, doubt the blueprint we've laid out, and even our own knowledge and internal dialogue fills us with loathing and uncertainty. Nietzsche called this the "hour of great contempt," and I'm sure many of you can relate.

During this time, lost in my own grim thoughts, I turned around, away from the ocean waves, and looked up at the moon, a slim crescent, but bright enough that the rest of the orb could be seen lightly, a lesser black against the ink-dark sky around it. I contemplated the moon, its cycles of waxing and waning, and considered that my own spirit was only "waned," which meant only that it must next wax. The halo around the moon reminded me of the serpent Ouroboros, the symbol of cyclical time, and the idea that I had been in this exact same head-space before, and would be again—these things are natural unavoidable, and in fact, desirous. They are a way of self auditing, checks and balances against our own ego, or value system, requiring that we delve deep and go to the dark places inside ourselves to see that devils still lurk there and must be faced.

I remembered the words from Joseph Campbell's "Hero With A Thousand Faces," pieces of which I had included in the earliest writing I had ever done for Operation Werewolf.

> *"The agony of breaking through personal limitations is the agony of spiritual growth. Art, literature, myth and cult, philosophy, and ascetic disciplines are instruments to help the individual past his limiting horizons into spheres of ever-expanding realization. As he crosses threshold after threshold, conquering dragon after dragon, the stature of the divinity that he summons to his highest wish increases, until it subsumes the cosmos. Finally, the mind breaks the bounding sphere of the cosmos to a realization transcending all experiences of form — all symbolizations, all divinities: a realization of the ineluctable void."*

We must all continue to conquer these dragons, in our continuous quest for personal ascendance and transformation. Conquering does not occur if we will not face ourselves. In these moments of blackness, we are engaged in a battle, and the dragons we face are called Fear, or Doubt, Anger, Illusion, and Limitation. Our sword is faith—an unshakable belief in what we are doing, and the connection thereof to a greater mythological framework that our lives grow around like vine on a trellis. Without that trellis, the vines will be condemned to crawling along the ground, but with it, they will flourish in the rays of the eternal :S:un.

As the battle turned, and I stood with my foot in the throat of that devil I faced, two meteors fell from opposite directions in a perfect "V" crossing one another just beneath the moon and disappearing into the void forever. I had been unaware that I was walking beneath the Geminid meteor shower, and even after that discovery, to me, this was a symbol, an undeniable sign from the heavens themselves that my path was :T:rue, and one with heart.

Upon returning home, I drew a sketch of the path of those meteors, crossing like an X beneath the waning December crescent moon, the *hagal* rune of the Younger Futhark in the middle, the "wolf rune" above, symbolizing the 13 lunar cycles of the year, and transition, consciousness, the spinal column. Around the moon, the serpent Ouroboros, present also in the Totenwolf design on the back patch of Operation Werewolf.

Our myth occurs where we pay attention to it. Where we foster it, and what direction we encourage its growth. Don't close your eyes on the world with all its awe and wonder and confirmation of your place in a story worth telling.

You might miss it.

FIGVRA XCII.

The **self-made king** is better than one who simply waited for a crown. **Tiwaz** is the heavy weight that comes along with that crown, the **knowledge** that the only underlying truth in the **cosmos** is the one **we have decreed for ourselves**, a pathway that leads straight as an arrow to our highest goal.

***

✝Failure is not Weakness✝

Recently, someone on my Instagram page asked a solid question.

> *"I know that you aren't perfect, and you must fuck up like all of us do.*
>
> *How do you deal with personal failure and shortcomings, and is failure always weakness?"*

The first line is of course true—I am far from perfect, and I feel at times like a I "fuck up" and fail frequently—whether by dropping the ball on one discipline or another, plans falling through, a business strategy not working out, or otherwise.

However, I believe that there is a massive difference between acknowledging failure, and thinking of yourself as "a failure." One is an expression of self-pity, or giving in to feelings of worthlessness, creating reality and self-fulfilling prophecy by speaking things into existence. The other is the byproduct of attempting challenging things with a high regularity—placing yourself in the "deep end" of life, instead of being content to dip your toes in. When we are constantly trying to crack open the longbones of this life and get at the very marrow of existence, we will put ourselves in harm's way, undergo trial and ordeal, and ultimately, sometimes, we will fail.

People who never fail are likely ones who ask very little of themselves.

Failure is only a weakness if after failing, you stop attempting to succeed—this is lasting failure, true defeat. A relinquishing of the internal fire and will, the grit and determination and tenacity we see outlined in the form of the :URUZ: rune—a rune which for me has one meaning of "never give :u:p."

If instead, we learn to hate failure like a cancer that is attempting to murder all the things we love and desire in our lives—hate it with a pure and righteous flame, born of the love of victory and self-overcoming—we turn it into a learning tool, and a motivator, rather than a conquering force.

We should all hate to fail, because it is a symptom if our inadequacies. But we should also learn from it. What can it teach us about ourselves? How has it showed us a flaw in the tapestry, a hole in our game, a weak point through which the enemy can storm the fortress? These are lessons hard learned and hard earned, but some of the most valuable experiences we will ever go through.

There is also the more ignominious kind of failure—those small, daily struggles that we lose to ourselves or our environment. These sorts of failures are the knife that truly cuts the throat of our greater selves, and leads to the really big failures along the road. They occur when we surrender to our baser selves, what I call our "thrall" mind, which always seeks the path of least resistance, the easy way, the road of comfort and laziness.

This is the voice heard when one begins bargaining with themselves. One last cigarette. Just a few more minutes in bed. An extra cheat meal. One less rep than the goal. It starts with showing you the easy way, and then starts to try to convince you, cajole, haggle and hassle.

> "If I smoke a cigarette now, I'll run an extra mile tomorrow."

> "OK, I'll sleep 10 more minutes, but I'll make sure I take time in the evening to do what I was going to do this morning."

> "Sure, I'll have this cheat meal, but I'll work it off on the treadmill."

STOP. RESET. NO YOU FUCKING WON'T.

Shut that voice down and make the strong choice, because you will absolutely not keep up your end of the bargain. You've already lost. You've already chosen the easy path, and taken one more action to reinforce the weaker part of your being, instead of the stronger part. You've turned up the volume on your thrall mind by one click, and reduced the volume on the voice that wants to make you a king.

This thrall mind is a terrorist, and the bombs he detonates are in the structures of your daily discipline, your work ethic, your duty and loyalty and honor. The thrall mind, when given the reins, will make you weak. A self-willed failure. Do not negotiate. Shut it down. Get mad. Silence that fucker and sacrifice your lower self to your higher Self. This is the mystery of Odin, when he says "myself to my own self given." A bloody act of devotion on the altar of personal transcendence and transformation, it is the giving of real power to yourself by reinforcing and feeding the higher self, the ultimate version of you that you want to be.

Make the strong choice. It's always the right choice.

+Aesthetic+

"I don't want to be a product of my environment. I want my environment to be a product of me." These words open the film "The Departed," one of my favorite Scorsese movies, spoken by the character Frank Costello, and Irish mob boss.

The words resonated with me strongly when I first heard them, and have stuck with me for years. I felt like this was the perfect delivery of a truth I had always believed and held as one of the major principles of self-creation.

If we are living lives of mythic action, our every word and deed becomes a spell of creation or destruction—shaping the malleable fabric of the world around us, changing our environment to reflect where our will is applied, and how. Gandhi famously said "be the change you want to see in the world," a statement often seen on Pinterest styled bumper stickers on soccer mom's vans, or bright eyed hipster idealists rusted beaters. Cliche, but only because almost all statements of basic truth seem that way through overuse and under-application.

In order to "be this change," one must apply consistent, consonant pressure in the direction he wants to see that change. By consonant, a word I use often, I mean that it has to "make sense together." Like notes in a music scale, or a well done painting, your actions must find congruence in order to become as effective as possible.

Consider it: what is a more sound strategy in war? Focused, tactical strikes at high-yield targets that eliminate them with brutal efficiency, or random squads sent out in all directions to take potshots into the trees, hoping they hit something?

In order for our lives to achieve this consonance, we must begin to view our life as a whole—as an artist looks at a canvas, or a sculptor his block of stone. From here, we should consider our lives as a work of art in motion, and shape it in a way that has a narrative, a direction—many elements working together in a flow toward some kind of completion. The idea of goals, and plotting the steps toward these goals is certainly one way to achieve this, but on a more visceral level, attaining consonance is done through aesthetic.

The word's definition is given as "a set of principles underlying and guiding the work of a particular artist or artistic movement." This view of aesthetic permeates the entirety of a life, and when we think of individuals who typify certain concepts or ideals, we are thinking of them as archetypes, or paragons of a certain aesthetic. Their lives have become "a line of poetry, written with a splash of blood."

Choosing an aesthetic is a crucial element of building your own legend, the framework within which you will operate, the filter through which you will see the world around you, and the body with which you will interact with that world.

The highest principle of humankind is to create.

It is the way in which we imitate the gods, and emulate the impulse they experienced when they created us in the myriad mythologies of humanity, spread across the aeons.

So many human beings sleepwalk through life, unaware or not stopping to consider and develop these ideas into something that can make their life more than what it is—a sweeping saga of their principles and ideals writ large on the stones of human history. No one wants to be forgotten, although we are all likely damned to that same grim fate—but we have the choice to attempt the mythic, the timeless, to strive for higher things, even if our outcome is sealed.

In Norse mythology, the gods walk to their final battle aware of the outcome, but choosing to perform the duty for its own sake. That, as Spengler might say, is what it means to be a thoroughbred.

To achieve aesthetic and consonance in our lives, we must begin by choosing one to embody.

In writing, they often tell you to fake a voice, or use someone else's until you find your own, and the same holds true here.

This is why the stories of the many gods and legends of our various peoples exist—to give us archetypes, not simply to revere, but to emulate— to actually spend each day attempting to become them with everything that this implies.

There is so much strength in this practice: losing one's temper, or making a poor dietary choice becomes so much more removed, or seems so much lesser to us when we are waking each day and choosing to embody a legendary archetype, a specific aesthetic.

We begin to view our lives as "a set of principles," rather than a random collection of meaningless actions. The environment around us too, should be considered. If we are building ourselves into a monolith of ideals that guide us as sure as a compass point, how can we apply this creative impulse elsewhere?

Obviously, we can do this through a host of actions, such as honing the crafts of writing, engineering, art, music, carpentry, but we can also begin to reinforce our aesthetic in our immediate surroundings by bringing first our physical form into agreement with our stated aims.

When one considers Achilles, Thor, Hanuman—he does not think of a couch-locked, skinny-fat form, atrophied through years of poor diet and sedentary living. Our emphasis on the ideas of physical training and healthy lifestyle come from many positive principles, but this is their quintessential one:

We cannot emulate the gods in a neglected body.

Beyond our bodies, our domiciles and places of work or training—how can we better bring them into alignment with this aesthetic we have chosen, in order to increase a harmonious interaction between increasing areas of our life?

One can begin to see this architecture grow and expand, as we can no longer neglect our immediate surroundings, but must cultivate them like a garden of the soul. Our dwelling-places and studies, our gyms and our work areas are where we spend many of our waking hours. Why should they not become temples to the Work, visual reminders of who and what we are seeking to become?

This practice becomes the weave of our own developing mythology as our strength grows, our practice becomes ritualized, our ritual becomes bedrock—the transformations within transform what is without, and ever widening ripples emanate outward from the core of our being into the material world, penetrating and transmuting raw elements and material. This is how men become symbols, what I have called "living runes," and from there can aspire to pass into legend.

Every action is a lesser or greater degree of one that came before it. If we can change ourselves, we can change the world.

The Inner Circle

✠Progressive Overload✠

Most people who have done some kind of weight training before are probably familiar with the legendary story of Milo of Croton—the Greek strongman who, as a child, began lifting the family calf overhead each day. As the calf grew, so did Milo, and by the time he was a man, he was doing his overhead presses with a full-sized bull.

This is essentially a fable detailing the theory of "progressive overload," which means gradually increasing the demands placed on the musculoskeletal system in order to stimulate an increase in strength, stamina, muscle growth and so on. In weightlifting terms, if start out deadlifting 135 pounds, we can enact progressive overload in one of three ways: by increasing the amount of reps performed, increasing the amount of weight at which the same reps are performed, or decreasing the amount of rest time between sets.

This makes it essential that we pay attention to where we are, and where we are trying to go, just as in all other aspects of life—if we can't remember how long our rest periods were last week when we trained the deadlift, how will we make progress? This randomness in approach is ineffective and lazy, and a lack of focus and attention to detail is a bacteria that will spread throughout our days and months, weakening and attacking our discipline and performance.

Progressive overload is not something that should be limited to our time in the gym. One of the oft-repeated maxims of Operation Werewolf is "physical training is never just physical." These methods and ways of thinking are infinitely transferable, and since we are always looking for more consonance in our lives, it doesn't make sense to draw these boundaries between important facets of our practice.

When we first begin training with weights, pushing up that first 135 pound bench press, it seems inconceivable to us that we could ever perform a rep with 200 more pounds on the bar. But slowly and surely, with right action and dedication in the gym, and the kitchen, we will creep inexorably towards that reality.

When I first began making the transition into self-employment, the amount of increased workload was staggering. Wasn't this supposed to be easier? I realized in short order that becoming one's own boss is a sacrifice of ease and comfort as surely as any other hardship or ordeal. I spent nearly all of my waking hours in the pursuit of attaining that freedom, step by incremental step, learning as I went, making mistakes, feeling I had "plateau'd," and even at some times stumbling and briefly wishing I could just go back to "working a regular job."

I kept the faith and the dedication. I accepted that this was where I had chosen to be, and put my head down and did the work, "put in the reps," as it were, and discovered that gradually, the workload seemed to become more manageable.

Some of this was certainly learning more effective ways to do things, cutting down on the time spent on things that at first seemed monolithic and were now mere foothills—but mostly, it was because I became acclimated to the increase in workload.

Just as 135 on the bench for me is now a light warmup on the way to a top set at 350 or so, the daily beat-down at the beginning of self employment is now a doable challenge that I enjoy. I am capable of taking on more responsibility and expanding my operations—but each time, I remember the story of Milo, and do it little by slow.

A cardinal sin of progressive overload is attempting it too fast, or recklessly. A surefire way to fail at a new endeavor is by taking on too much at one time. We should certainly always be ambitious in our selection of weights, reps, workload and so on, but we should never be ignorant of our own limitations. Sometimes it can pay to roll the dice, but steady movement forward beats relying on luck.

In our personal life, we can view this as not taking on too many new disciplines at once. Instead of trying to completely reorganize your life all in one sweeping action, change one thing. Create a habit of it. Maintain the habit. Select another. Same goes for business. Don't become "like butter scraped over too much bread," by dividing your resources into multiple directions all at the same time. Focus on one thing, get good at it, make sure it's delivering and working like a well-oiled machine, then put feelers out in a new, complimentary territory.

That certain, irrefutable forward movement will eventually put you in a place where you can look back with disbelief at how far you've come, instead of looking forward with uncertainty at how far you have to go.

One step at a time, taken indomitably in the same direction, forever.

✠Mannaz and Mantra✠

Most who are aware of Operation Werewolf are similarly aware of my interest in runes, both on a linguistic and historical level, as well as their application as a sort of psychological wrench—a mental and spiritual tool used for specific and repeatable purpose.

Before we continue, because of language limitations and misconceptions, it is necessary to define what I mean when I use the word "spiritual:"

> *"In its simplest terms, when we use this word, we will be referring to the intangible thing within man which can be seen as the seat of his character, emotions, and connection with the*

unseen world around him. Also, his will, and other such unquantifiable concepts that man has felt, interacted with, and experienced, knows to be real, but cannot show in a physical form—but certainly can see the effects of.

Just as we cannot see "love" as anything beyond an assortment of chemicals in the brain, but can witness it in a mother's devotion to her son, or a man's to his wife; just as we cannot see "will" as chemical combination or a physical form, we can witness it in the determination of a mountain climber, a monk setting his body on fire, or even someone resisting the addiction of cigarettes or narcotics—we cannot see the "soul" or "spirit" of a man, or his "character," but we can see the change they create in the world about him."

—from 'The Werewolf Manifesto,' available in print from Operation Werewolf Spring 2018

Just as this term 'spiritual' is representative of an intangible, the runes themselves are intangibles, gigantic conceptual glaciers and mountains—titanic architectures of thought and experience that have become inseparable from my worldview through long use. A rune, simply put, is a letter in an alphabet—but it is so much more than this in the same way that the ocean is different from a glass of salt water.

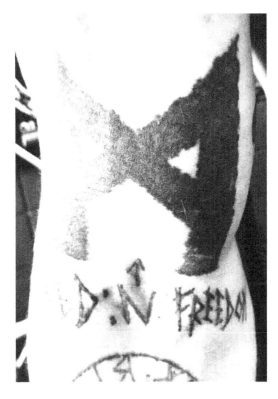

One of the runes tattooed on my body is a large "Mannaz" on my right bicep. Mannaz is a word from the theoretical proto Indo-European language, from which the word "man" is derived, denoting man as a collective, "mankind," and also the individual himself. Some scholars make the connection between *mannaz and the root words *men- (to think, as in, "mentality"), connecting the idea of man defining himself as a "thinker," or a being of consciousness and thought. The Sanskrit word (a language that comes from the same root) *manas* has shaped my understanding of the Mannaz rune in many crucial ways, and whether or not linguistic scholars accept or deny the etymological connection between "man" and "mind," the philosophical connection remains.

Manas is one of the four parts of the mind in Hindu thought, representing the faculty that with the help of the sensory organs, receives information from the world around us and presents it the intellect. It is the instinctive mind, as well as the individualizing principle that allows man to see himself as an individual, separate from the collective. It is the seat of desire, as well, that undisciplined aspect of self that creates and moves us toward actions for the sake of satiating ourselves in some way or another.

It is divided into two parts, the *"buddhi manas"* and the *"kama manas"* which refer to the "higher mind" and the "lower mind," another idea that has resonated strongly with me and been discussed often in my writing. Even in the shape of the *Mannaz rune, we can see two separate vertical lines "communicating" with one another with a kind of "wiring" that goes from one to the other and crosses in the center, creating a pictogram of balance, interconnectedness, and exchange.

The rune itself also indicates the idea of man in his highest potential—what he is ultimately capable of if he is performing at the greatest level possible through training the lower mind to be ruled by the higher mind. One of the techniques through which this can be encouraged is that of mantra. The word itself connects to the subject at hand, and is a Sanskrit word made up of the root, *manas*, and the suffix *-tra*, denoting a tool or instrument. Taken together, a "mind tool," or "instrument of consciousness."

In the runic tradition, formulas are created from various runes, and sung in a practice called "galdr," which refers to the vocal nature of it, often seemingly gibberish words strung together for an initiatic meaning that only reveals itself through the repetition of the galdr. Mantra refers to this same practice, and by its definition, was seen as a tool for training the mind in a certain direction, or to change the thought process by controlling it in a specific way.

In short, one way of looking at mantra is words and sounds designed to produce something in one's mind. What that something is depends on the mantra itself, as well as the individual's intention.

Applying this to our personal practice is an incredibly powerful method of quite literally altering our brains and consciousness in a similar way to how the body is shaped and altered during deliberate physical training. The study of neuroplasticity has proven that brain activity is changed through practices such as mediation, but also suggests that it is possible that physical changes occur in the brain itself through training it via these "instruments of thought." We also know that physical exercise produces an increase in grey matter volume in multiple regions of the brain, proving that what we do, and the activities we engage in, alter the very seat of our cognitive abilities.

Scientists have also proven that when we think or feel a certain way, neurons fire together, connect and begin to create a "neurological pathway." The first time we think to ourselves "I am weak, I can't do this," for example, we can see it as walking through an untamed frontier, a difficult and arduous journey from one place to another, cutting through undergrowth and foliage, fording rivers, ultimately arriving at our destinations as trailblazers. The second time, a beaten path begins to appear, and the river fords are built into bridges. By the hundredth time, roads are being built, and train track is being laid, until some time in the future, flying cars are smoothly navigating the highways at blink of an eye speeds.

What this means is that the more times we give in to a negative thought or emotion, self-defeating internal talk, a difficult workout makes us quit— we are making it easier for ourselves to do or feel that in the future. This is not some white-light, hippie talk. This is scientific fact— the more we perform an action, but more importantly, think a thought, we cast a vote for more of the same. We lay down an infrastructure to build up that area of our brain.

This is why it becomes so vitally important for us to train to control our emotional responses to things early and often. Habits become difficult to break, modes of thinking or dealing with our problems become such monumental tasks, because we have spent years building that "muscle" in our mind, until we are fighting a 300 pound sumo wrestler each time we try to not fly off the handle when we can't find our phone (something I've been guilty of many times!).

This is where mantra comes in.

Developing the correct neurological pathways means treating the brain as a muscle and applying the same principles here that we would in the gym, or on the mats. Repetitive, consistent, correct training to achieve results. My jiu jitsu coach is fond of saying "practice doesn't make perfect, practice just makes habit. Perfect practice makes perfect." We can't just throw ourselves into something haphazardly, we need an organized training routine.

My suggestion is that you start simple. There's no need to learn another language, or pick up an entirely new verbiage in order to get started—although the study of language, traditional mantra and galdr is certainly a rewarding endeavor. Instead, begin by identifying a specific aspect of yourself that you are looking to get control over. In simple terms, this could be a lack of discipline getting out of bed in the morning, or a habit of losing your temper easily.

You will create (and keep to yourself, for now), a mantra that identifies this by applying a positive approach. It could be something as simple as, "I am in control of myself and my emotions. My temper is a product of my lower self, and I am its master. I am calm, rational, and powerful." There isn't a need for flowery words or poetics, although if this helps you connect with the process, by all means, go for it. What we are looking to achieve here is the creation of small, simple tool to begin creating the pathway in your mind in a direction that will prove corrective for the problem you are dealing with.

While you recite your mantra, you will also keep firmly in mind that each time you master your temper, you are building a habit. Each time you give in, you are doing the same. If you master it next time, applying your mantra, being in control, calm, cool, powerful, and so on, you are weakening the neurological pathway that is lit up when your temper flares. By doing it time after time, each success makes it less likely that you will lose your temper next time.

Success is a habit, as surely as anything else. We create it through developing a practice.

Going forward, each month, when the Inner Circle comes out, I will be presenting one rune each time, with a bit of information on its meaning, application and suggested meditation for it. You can apply these in your creation of personal mantras and "words of power," that you can begin to see as tools—the kettle bells and barbells of the consciousness, affecting change there just as certainly as in all other forms of our training, *mannaz and *mantra* working together to build a complete human in the image we have chosen.

☦Jera and Yantra☦

This time, we are going to continue the work begun, and focus on another runic concept and its correlation.

Just as we looked at the linguistic connection between :MANNAZ: and Mantra, this time we are exploring two other similar words and ideas, the :JERA: rune and yantra, a Sanskrit word that translates literally as "machine/contraption."

To oversimplify, the word yantra generally refers nowadays to a symbol with mystical properties used in meditation or to adorn walls and floors of temples. Each yantra has its own specific use and purpose.

Its older meaning is perhaps more interesting, and comes from the root yam- "to sustain, support, fasten," connected with the suffix -tra just like "mantra." Those who read last month's issue might remember that this suffix indicates a tool or instrument. Taken together, "a sustaining instrument," "a fastening tool," "a support system."

At its deeper core, the yantra is a machine for generating energy toward a specific purpose. Most of what people are familiar with when they think of yantras are brightly colored geometric devices on cloth or metal, covered in markings, sometimes numbers, usually letters and other "mantras." Coded information, placed into the visual realm in order to produce a result. Where mantra is aural, yantra is visual—mantra is vibratory, and yantra is dynamic, moving, energetic.

If a mantra is a thought-form, then a yantra is the structure in which it resides, or in other words, if a mantra were to represent a god, then the yantra is the temple or dwelling-place of that god.

Looking at the :JERA: rune, we see something different right away in its form—it is the only one of the 24 of the Elder Futhark that is not "connected." Rather, it is made up of two separate parts, engaging one another in what appears to be a rotational dance, bringing to mind the endless spinning of a dynamo or generator. It is no surprise then, that the word is the root for our "year," and "hour," its meaning illuminated even further when one considers the Germanic (and Indic) concept of the year as a rotation of seasons, and even time itself as cyclical in nature, and not linear.

This cyclical movement and dance is also reminiscent of the tandava, Shiva's dance of creation and destruction, a manifestation of primal rhythmic energy. This is essentially what :JERA: is symbolic of—the rhythm of the year, the seasons, the solar wheel and the lunar one, spinning endlessly throughout the eons, and man's place within it all. The :JERA: rune is also set in the very middle of the Elder rune row, right next to :EIHWAZ:, the rune of vertical expansion, and consciousness, where :JERA: is horizontal and belongs to the realms of being and becoming.

:JERA: is a symbol that holds the meaning of "harvestable energy," or available resources, and in this way is very similar to the concept of a yantra—it is the power that can be drawn upon to sustain, to support, if one puts in the proper time and devotion. Dedicated work in the fields, sweat, and labor leads to a good harvest.

Similarly, a yantra by itself, simply viewed, does not produce much energy. It is the time spent with it, exploring it, understanding its hidden meanings and information and initiating ourselves into the language and circuitry of it. The more time we spend in contemplation of the runes, or the recitation of mantra, or the engagement of our mental faculties with the intricate systems of yantra or sigil—the more they weave and connect themselves through our mind, evoking specific modes of being within us through their continued dedicated use.

To use another example, many writers I know use a specific pen for a specific purpose. This pen is the one they use when experiencing writers block, or having a completely "off" day. It takes on a talismanic importance, and is saved up just for such times, separated from mundane use. It is never grabbed when they just need something to write with. It serves a very clear and specific function. The more times it is used for this function, the stronger the bridge becomes between its use and this intended outcome. The "magic" pen gains a power all its own because of the time and experience investment.

As Craig Williams said to me during a discussion on the topic (someone I consider that rare combination of both a friend and a teacher):

"The dead letters of the Mantra must be awakened and the hollow structure of the Yantra must be filled. This enlivening process occurs via the Fire of the Ritualized Life: the flesh, the blood, the bones and the breath must pulse with the heat of our dedication and devotion. Only then can we truly be Enlivened Beings! Two sacred fires are enkindled, one within the mantra/yantra, one within the mind-body of the devotee; both must burn wildly and without regret. These fires intermingle in alchemical chaos to birth our true Self."

The value of these things is not immediately clear to the uninitiated, because they always ask the question: "wouldn't it be more valuable to force your way through the writer's block, and simply do it "on your own?"

This misses the mark completely, and doesn't take into consideration the fact that human beings are symbolic, and they are creatures of ritual. We place importance on things "set aside" from daily use, and we venerate objects and give them importance because it is in our nature to do so.

Whether a "lucky jersey" worn during a big game, a pre-competition ritual by a wrestler, organizing one's personal space in a certain way, or creating sigils, runes, yantras—the human being is engaging in ritual.

When we dedicate time and invest ourselves in these things, we create "shortcuts" in our minds, and this is exactly what kind of machine a yantra is. Just as a car is a faster way to get from point A to point B, a yantra, a rune, or a sigil, is a faster way to take the brain and consciousness from point A to point B, in a specific, intended fashion.

A yantra is more complex than a single sigil or rune, and this is an important clarification—a single symbol generally contains similar information coded into it. For example, the :JERA: rune is tightly packed symbol with an immense amount of information within it, but all that information is related, and makes up one idea, writ large. Likewise, a basic sigil generally carries within it a specific concept or idea, relatively limited in scope. In some schools of thought, the more simple and basic the concept, the more effective the sigil.

A yantra, by contrast, is made up of many symbols, all working together to form a massive structure of energetic correspondences, all of them working toward specific ends within a greater whole. For another example, if a sigil is a letter, a yantra is a word. If a rune is a crown, a yantra is king, court and country. These ideas defy language in the same way that time or dreams are difficult to define or box up neatly.

Perhaps the easiest way for us to understand these things is to consider that humans themselves are living yantras.

A machine, by definition, is a grouping of pieces that operate together in unison to perform a specific function, or set of functions. In this regard, the human body and brain together make up the most complex machine yet discovered in the universe. A system containing myriad intricate smaller systems that work together to produce energy, motion, thought, electricity, action, consciousness—the sum of all that we can do or know resides within this incredible framework of our nervous system and the body it lives within. But to what end, or purpose?

I have, in the past, referred to individuals highly engaged with the process of self-creation as "living runes." By this, I mean that an individual, through the course of his life, by identifying strongly with certain principles or aesthetics, becomes something greater than a simple human being. Perhaps the highest goal in this life is to typify a concept so strongly that one becomes a paragon of his ideals, an emulatable archetype of that which he has dedicated his life to.

He is capable of constructing himself, through force of will and intention and consonance, into a monolithic set of symbols and harmonized principles that might tower beyond his death. That formation might then be witnessed by those who come after, to strengthen, to inspire, and like a spiritual generator unaffected by the passage of time—to energize.

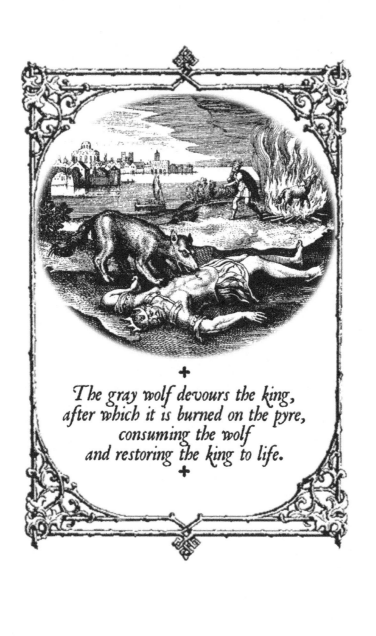

*The gray wolf devours the king,
after which it is burned on the pyre,
consuming the wolf
and restoring the king to life.*

✛Resistance✛

Make no mistake—we are involved in a war.

This one isn't being fought in some foreign theater far away, but right here, right now—in every Hollywood movie, every comedian's witty joke, every carefully scripted news story, celebrity social media post, and in every corner of the internet and urban sprawl alike, the bullets are flying.

We've said from the beginning that Operation Werewolf means rabid resistance—this resistance that we have built up is like an immune system that allows us to exist with no adverse effect in a world of bacteria, virus, plague and pestilence.

Immunity to the weakness that pervades this society. Immunity to the drab—to the boring and banal. Unaffected and unmoved by the incessant gospel of mediocrity and sameness that these false prophets of the grey concrete wasteland are screaming from every minaret of this rotting Empire.

This resistance comes at a cost—when you are resistant to sameness, they will call you a bigot. When you resist the destruction of that which is beautiful and strong, they will call you hateful.

They call convictions phobias. They call love hate.

They call slavery freedom. They call ignorance strength. They make a desolation, and call it peace.

Because this is the root of what our enemies want: a desolation of sameness. A world in which all thoughts are policed, all actions and words and beliefs and books and music and art scrutinized under the lens of the current narrative of doublethink and historical revisionism. All that does not agree is razored out, changed, twisted, and made "safe."

In this desolation they seek to cause, every citizen is an aspiring warden, a guard, a snitch, a rat. They do so willingly, to be applauded for their virtue, which they signal by rooting out these dangerous thinkers—these terrorists who dare to speak freely or challenge the narrative. They title themselves rebels or anarchists, while they report these transgressions to their superiors in positions of power.

This living cesspool is hugely impressed with its own positions and conditioned beliefs, and they howl their self-approval into the echo chamber of modern society.

But something is happening:

As they attempt to make and control both the future and the past, they are failing. Their attempts to censor and silence are becoming more ineffective, and their impotence is audible in their wild shrieking and shouting down of anything that challenges their position.

They are failing in this war, because we who are the hammer to this monument of sickness are creatures born of myth and creation, might and merciless forward movement.

We are men and women of action, not reaction. We see their hatred for us, and we are not drawn down into the same depths of backbiting and gnashing of teeth. We will not be reconstructed into the shapeless forms they would make us into, and we will not fall in line.

And we are growing stronger.

They are making us stronger. Because although our resistance is one of immunity, one of disdain and disgust for the virus of modernity, theirs is born of resentment, and our every action and creation meets with this direct kind of resistance that seeks to tear down those things which it recognizes as a threat to itself.

Every time their demands are met with an artist or musician falling to their knees in supplication, they root these pitiful apologists from our ranks.

Every time they freeze our assets with the push of a button, we rally together and offer aid to our own, finding common ground with one another where they only see enemies.

Every time they remove an avenue for us, they force us to make a new road where none existed before.

Every time they make our life more difficult, they provide us with an opportunity to glory in our own ability to conquer, to achieve in the face of adversity. To turn their resistance into training, making us harder than life, as they grow softer and more reliant on the feeding tubes of mediocrity and ease.

We use their own weapons against them. We broadcast our black flag signal out across their own channels and airwaves, the pen doing the work that the sword cannot.

The printed page, dangerous art and music are all firing like machine guns and heavy artillery, their reports ringing out as a rallying cry to those of us still unafraid to speak our mind, to sacrifice our reputation in their world for notoriety and respect in our own.

We create our own culture from a vital interplay of traditional thought and value blended with realism and critical thinking while theirs feeds on its own excrement and yesterday's court jesters, immolating each of its own idols as new crusades and witch hunts leave none untouched.

This war is being waged.

Pick a side—for freedom or for empire. For thought control or untamed existence.

Because if you don't choose, the day will come when the choice is made for you, and in this battle, you are either with us, or against us.

FIGVRA XCII.

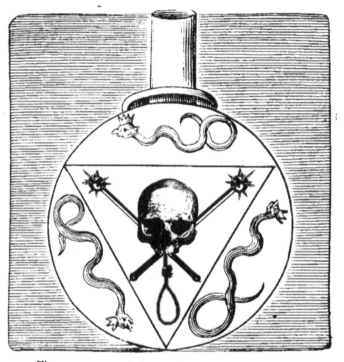

He is capable of constructing **himself**, through **force of will and intention and consonance**, into a monolithic set of **symbols** and harmonized principles that might tower beyond his **death**.

***

✠Standard Bearers✠

Operation Werewolf marches under the sign of the black banner which bears emblazoned on it a wolf skull and crossed bones, surrounded by a serpent, *Ouroboros*, the entirety of which we call the "Totenwolf," or "death-wolf."

Many have chosen to cast this symbol aside for their own, using the tenets and ideas discovered through Operation Werewolf, as well as the network, to build their own tribes under their own banners, renaming and re-creating the same general method with that spirit of individuality and separation that men naturally crave.

Although I see the perceived value in this, and call many of these men and their tribes my friends, allies, and associates, this action in many ways has missed the mark—overlooked one of the vital concepts around which the creation of Operation Werewolf was based: solidarity, and consonance.

From the Complete Zines, Volume 1: Iron and Blood Vol II:

> "Its symbolism is three-fold: Death, the Wolf, and the Serpent, who we call "the Spawn of the Ironwood." We use these ancient archetypes for their symbolic value in the current age, as well as the internal work we undergo.
>
> In order to create ourselves anew, we must destroy that which came before. The Spawn of the Ironwood are representative of those energies of destruction, the ending of cycles, the clearing away of old and corrupt forms of being and existing...

When we don the Death-wolf on our back, or fly its dread banner at our Division gatherings, we are hailing those principles that are the bloody death of our old ways of thinking, of doing, of living.

We are hailing our eternal march, grim and warlike, towards a greater destiny than that which would be chosen for us by those who wear the crowns of this earth.

We are signaling to others who are ready for something more, and calling them to our grisly standard. Werewolf Legions, unite!"

One of the reasons a standard is borne is for purposes of identification on a battlefield. A clear sign showing who allied forces are, to more effectively operate on the battlefield. For this reason, the intention at the beginning was that all those who stood under the flag of the Operation would stand under that same banner, a clear signal to friend and foe alike:

"We are united. We stand together as one."

However, as stated, the value of individual Divisions wearing their own standard became clear as a way for the "true" to separate themselves from the "rank and file," those who were perhaps flirting or dabbling with the symbolism but not understanding the life reform that is to come along with it.

This separation and distinction could possibly have been avoided with a different approach: that of internal correction.

It is true that anyone can put on a wolf-skin, but it does not make them a wolf.

At best, they are attacking the work with heart, in an honest effort to improve themselves, adhering to the tenets of this strength culture, connecting with others and forming lasting bonds that lead to the improvement of the whole—these kinds of men and women are increasing their own honor, and that of the Operation.

At worst, they are interlopers, embarrassments to the cause, interested in the trappings of this growing mythology, but not in the movement and personal transformation it requires. These are the worst kind of people, and we know their works—they are actively inhibiting the Operation, and working to destroy its reputation by way of their own weakness and lack of dedication or understanding.

In militaristic organizations of the past, being a standard bearer was considered an honor, and a privilege, and should still be seen as such—bearing the standard of Operation Werewolf comes along with a certain kind of danger, in that one willingly identifies themselves as a part of something that many are in opposition to. This opposition sees a standard bearer as a prime target.

Also, they open themselves up to challenge from within—from other bearers of the standard. This behavior should be encouraged. The Operation was never meant to be insular, or an edgy statement made by lone "wolves," but a living network of pressure, competition, and power.

Those who actively avoid this sort of face to face interaction and pressure should be pressured all the way out. Operation Werewolf is not for the faint of heart, nor for the lukewarm—it is for the extreme, the passionate, the aflame!

Those who are a vessel of holy fire—a breathing, bleeding temple built to the god called strength and overcoming.

The timid, the chronically mediocre and those who avoid confrontation and pressure must be rooted out before their cancer can spread.

We see Operation Werewolf as a living representation of the black sun, and the black sun as both a threshing floor and a pathway to the center. One begins at the outermost edge and works their way inward, toward becoming. Toward belonging. But the way to the center goes through the trials and tribulations of this overcoming, and the rays of the black sun are reaping blades!

> *"Lonely one, you are going the way to yourself! And your way goes past yourself, and past your seven devils! You will be a heretic to yourself and witch and soothsayer and fool and doubter and unholy one and villain. You must be ready to burn yourself in your own flame: how could you become new, if you had not first become ashes?"*

Those who wear the Totenwolf proudly should be flesh and blood symbols of its tenets and practices, physically strong and mentally sharp, capable, dangerous, moving ever toward the center of the black sun—and it should always be remembered that whatever the banner, we will know one another by our works!

+Bhagavan and Berkano+

Since these "paired word" articles seem to be becoming a continuing thing, I'd like to put a disclaimer at the beginning of this third installment.

I am not connecting words together in an implication that they always stem from a shared etymology. They are words that I've connected together poetically, or esoterically, and not necessarily from a linguistic approach, although when they I do make that connection, I try to "show my work."

As someone who studies language for the "pathways" I find it opens to interesting ideas, I am merely sharing some of these connections I've made, and believe that developing one's ability to synchronize and synthesize is a worthwhile characteristic of those who would become "bhagavan" themselves.

This month's pairing came as a product of considering the ideas behind an upcoming ritual I was planning with my brother Jack Donovan. In it, we would be honoring the Germanic deity Frey, or *Frajaz*, that is itself, like *bhagavan* a word that is more title than name, and simply means "Lord."

In applying the usual process I do when considering these things, I start by creating a sort of "tree" in my mind, and conceptualize things from the roots up, that is, beginning with deep meditations on the often "hidden" or occult primal ideas within which dwell the god forms and archetypes.

Instead of starting with the visible, it is often best to challenge oneself by considering the less obvious and more esoteric truths that lie within the known stories or lore about these gods.

Often times during these meditations, mysteries make themselves known in a sort of self initiation that is then realized and completed during the ritual itself.

From the roots, to the trunk, I begin to work my way through the visible, the applied experiences that might make up the day to day praxis of veneration or worship, or dedication to the god form.

In what activities, items, or lifestyles is this god observable?

The branches and leaves make up the various ways people have understood these ideas throughout time, and what forms they have taken, the words they have used to identify and give shape to it, through to the present day, where it often has deteriorated or degenerated, but sometimes still exists in potent forms with different names and titles.

Following this, the sap, or *ojas* of the entire structure—what can be done to vitalize it, to energize, regenerate, or bring viridity to it?

This sap is the ritual itself, but also the developing cult practices that flow through the god form and maintain its strength and bring new fire to the ancient, rather than "worshiping the ashes."

During these meditations, I am reminded of the Berkano rune, also called Bjarkan in the Younger Futhark.

It is a rune of growing things, certainly, but also of the passage of time, arising, being, passing away. The cycle of rot and renewal that is seen everywhere in the natural world.

Beyond these interpretations however, Berkano is also a rune of majesty, that contains within it the principles of the creative impulse, bringing forth ideas and manifesting them into the world of being and becoming.

In its rune poem, we read:

> *"Birch bears no fuit; yet without seed it brings forth shoots, for it is generated from its leaves. Splendid are its branches and gloriously adorned its lofty crown which reaches the sky."*

When considering the runes as a pathway, if Tiwaz can be seen as the rune of mastery through sacrifice, then Berkano can be looked at as the majesty and glory that arises from deep understanding of the temporal plane paired with creative vision, and the ability to see endeavors through to their fruition—from which stems abundance.

It is a rune displaying one of the necessary qualities of Lordship, the attainment of which can be seen as essential to the cult of Frajaz, whose name is something to be emulated and obtained.

On an impersonal level, however, it represents that godhead that exists without need of persona, the divine that exists in nature itself— the supreme and permeating energy that gives life and rhythm to the very cosmos.

Drawing from this concept, I began to think of nature itself as an idol, or a container through which man could understand the divine and how this correlated with the Berkano rune itself, and from there, that the true worship of nature is one of silent reflection on all of reality.

There is a Sanskrit term, Bhagavan, that is often translated as "idol." As is most often the case with language, a cursory glance is not enough to understand the various subtleties and pathways of a word, and so I dug deeper.

From this, I was drawn to the definition of the word from the Vishnu Purana, circa 1st century BCE:

> "That essence of the supreme is defined by the term Bhagavat. The word Bhagavat is the denomination of that primeval and eternal god: and he who fully understands the meaning of that expression, is possessed of holy wisdom, the sum and substance of the Vedas.
>
> The word Bhagavat is a convenient form to be used in the adoration of that supreme being, to whom no term is applicable; and therefore Bhagavat expresses that supreme spirit, which is individual,

almighty, and the cause of causes of all things.

The letter Bh implies the cherisher and supporter of the universe. By ga is understood the leader, impeller, or creator. The dissyllable Bhaga indicates the six properties, dominion, might, glory, splendour, wisdom, and dispassion. The purport of the letter va is that elemental spirit in which all beings exist, and which exists in all beings."

I felt this perfectly described my understanding of Berkano as the supporting energy of the universe, but from there, when I began to look at the term *bhaga*, found that it, like Frey/ Frajaz, translated often simply as "lord."

Going deeper, it is a term that indicates the "six properties," which are, in Sanskrit, a much more complex idea that we will delve into next month.

At the end of this month-long meditation on these things, I found myself at the Wolves' land in Cascadia, Waldgang, facing a brightly adorned altar on which sat the cult image of Frajaz himself.

Antlers, boar skulls, and an abundance of coins from all over the world piled around him, the flowers spattered with blood from the day's offerings.

Torchlight played across this scene, and I drank deeply of fresh blood mixed with a strong drink, and addressed my brothers and guests.

That night, during and after the ritual, we celebrated the strength of earthly pleasures, mastering temporal wealth and power, and the different aspects of kingship and might, and I felt the sap quickening in the ancient tree of the Cult of the Lord of this World.

+Bhagavan and Berkano pt.ii: 'Becoming Bhagavan'+

In Vedic literature, to be called *bhagavan*, is to be possessed of six qualities. The possession of these qualities are pre-requisite for being an excellent leader, and those who walk the path of the Lord, Frajaz, and look for rulership in this world would do well to learn and attain them.

Like the disclaimer in the first part of this article from last month, I am by no means an expert in the Sanskrit language, nor do I present myself as one. These translations, thoughts and understandings of terminologies stem from a study of the word definitions as shown by

Sanskrit dictionaries and etymological information, filtered through my own worldview and experience.

Jnana

The first quality is jnana, often translated simply as "knowledge." A leader must have a kind of knowledge separate simply from "book learning," or theoretical information gained from the acquisition of fact and statistic.

He must cultivate that knowing that is enmeshed in the true reality of things, uncluttered with conditioned ways of thinking and personal prejudice. His understanding of the world around him must be perennial, total, divine in its scope.

That kind of knowing and knowledge must be distilled from years of experience placed under the lens of deep reflection and openness to change, a lack of attachment to subjective belief systems and dogmas.

Jnana cannot come from "crash courses" nor the premature enlightenment that stems from those would-be leaders who place the cart in front of the horse in regards to real authority and wisdom. It is the knowledge of reality itself.

Bala

From the Proto-Indo-European *bel*, for "strength, power."

The subtleties that came to be associated with the word are more accurately described as "viridity," a sort of vigorous endurance capable of going the distance. It is also the understanding of how and when to exert force in the right direction, as well as a physical, phallic kind of energy.

The leader must have force to exert, and this force must not be limited to proxy, but an indwelling might that is both intimidating and reassuring. When it must be, it can be articulated in various ways, depending on the situation.

A good leader doesn't lash out—he sees where the point of maximal effect is, and strikes there, with great force and precision.

Ishvara

From a compound word that translates literally as "to be capable of/ownership of the best kind of choices, or rulership."

Ishavara is, simply put, having the characteristics of a ruler to begin with. It is rulership itself, the definition of a king in all that implies.

More than this, it is a recognition of that higher self that becomes the personal god of the ruler or leader, his own heightened consciousness that he can call upon for aid or counsel.

It is the higher self that rules the individual, and is submitted to in favor of those who succumb to their base desires or personal wants and needs in order to serve a greater purpose.

This principle of understanding that the higher consciousness knows what is best for the body is a fundamental concept of rulership in general, and it must be practiced and internalized first on an individual basis before it can ever be brought to bear on others.

The personal Ishvara is not dissuaded nor conquered by hardship or ordeal, and carries the ruler through life's most violent storms.

Virya

From whence comes the words *virtus*, virtue, virile, and so on.

Virya is masculinity, and all that goes with the true expression of it. It is testosterone, personified.

The heroic attitude of the conqueror that is needed by all strong rulers or leaders of men, and the willingness to gladly engage in wholesome and challenging activities.

It is right action, not just action for its own sake, and it is discharged in the manliest of fashions. It is direct, and encompassing, like an army arrayed on the field.

Confidence, and a positive mindset that will weather high stress and tense situations and remain impassive and ready to do what is necessary.

Duty, responsibility, and loyalty fall under the aegis of virya as well, and all things that are inherently masculine and noble.

Shakti

A powerful man understands the feminine nature of things as well, and also is capable of the act of creation. Not of children from the womb, but of ideas, empires, works of art and literature.

He is someone who can bring something from the realm of raw potential into a fully realized state that changes the world around him, changes lives, changes minds and thoughts and feelings. He is a magician.

Shakti is the ability to act dynamically, to understand the value of fluidity and necessary compromise. It is the power to move through the universe and present what is needed for any situation. To "be like water."

A ruler must be a creative, or he will lack the imagination to inspire, or to see past his own motivations and rigid mindset.

Tejas

Its word roots mean things like "heat, shine, endure, illuminate," and also "fire."

Tejas is the internal inferno from whence a great man draws his boundless strength and passion.

It is also that intangible without which a leader cannot exist: charisma.

It is the brightly burning flame that draws those around him to him, and makes them desire to follow him, or to be near him.

We have all felt its impact on ourselves, but possibly struggled to identify just what it is that defines the idea of someone who is charismatic, ut it is there, simple, easy to see.

Tejas is fire, and humans all wish to stand near it. With these six qualities, a man might rule the world.

☩RUNES: Pathways to Mastery☩

I've discussed in the past the concept of looking at the runes as a pathway to mastery, to rulership, both of the self and the world around you. In the first eight runes of the Elder Futhark, we can see some of the root principles needed to walk the heroic road—information needful to those individuals who would set themselves apart from the rank and file and become men of power.

In the second eight, cosmic foundations are laid—eternal truths of how the world works, and how consciousness interacts within it. Massive ideas of cosmology and cosmogony, necessary to understand by those looking to shatter the myopic worldview of linear time and other man—made limitations.

By the third, we are looking at runes of mastery. Rulership, kingdom—that which is attained by seeking the solar crown.

𝕿𝖎𝖜𝖆𝖟 is often referred to as the rune of sacrifice and law, and while this is so, there are other, more esoteric meanings that can be derived from it. Tiwaz is also a man's chosen destiny—the pathway and blueprint he has laid out for himself, created from his own past actions and words, and set himself on a course for.

The self-made king is better than one who simply waited for a crown. Tiwaz is the heavy weight that comes along with that crown, the knowledge that the only underlying truth in the cosmos is the one we have decreed for ourselves, a pathway that leads straight as an arrow to our highest goal. Discovering that pathway to our True North is the first part of the great work of our existence, and walking it to its end is the second. True kings of this world will walk that path without deviation or distraction.

BERKANO has been discussed already earlier in this issue, and refers both to grasping the primordial ideas of being and becoming, but another direction is that of an individuals "forest of power." A ruler, or a man of power, extends a great forest around himself that is made of both deed and fame, charisma, network, and area of effect.

His sphere of influence can tell a great deal about him, and those who would claim authority and rulership in this world are never seen without it, whether large or small. At the beginning of his road, a man's forest is only a few saplings, devoid of canopy and unable of providing much.

The developed ruler has spread those woods far and wide, and other men exist within its edges, dwelling there on what resources are created by it. This contains within itself the idea of patronage, and the assistance and backing a ruler can provide for those who are in his territory. Generosity, open-handedness, and all the concepts of lordly wealth are here also.

EHWAZ, the horse. Here we see the importance of partnership, the ability to work together for mutual benefit, symbiosis, and the ability to choose the correct "pony to bet on."

It is a man's ability to be a good judge of "horseflesh," or his uncanny knack at seeing human behaviors and predicting outcomes.

If Berkano is influence, Ehwaz can be seen to compliment it as "reputation." The strongest thing a man can ride into battle is a warhorse built from reputation and his word. Ehwaz encompasses agreements, business dealings and so on, and can be seen as a form of "horse trading," where cattle will suffice for a more common man.

𝔈𝔥𝔴𝔞𝔷 is a crucial bedrock for the ruler to understand that without his men, he is no ruler. It is also his ability to bring out the best in people, to "create men" himself, which is the mark of only the absolute best of leaders.

Mannaz is about being able to make men want to follow you, rather than simply commanding them to do so through artificial means or buying their loyalty. It encompasses interpersonal communication and close relationships, as well as maximizing potential, ownership, and tying men together into teams.

Being a ruler can be something of a lonely lifestyle as well, and this rune symbolizes that separation between a ruler and the rest of humanity—not many are called to rule, and as such, it places them in a position without the same comradery as others enjoy.

All power comes at a price.

LAGUZ is flow, fluidity, energy, the ability to "be like water." It is also a critically important ability to see all energy as the same thing, and to see currencies of all kinds as one sort of electrical current through which a ruler is able to influence and affect the world.

Everything is a circuit board, and all those circuits are tripped and charged by current. There are many different kinds of currency: money, obviously, but also fear, respect, love, favors, debt, and so on. All of these can be seen as a ruler's outward "flow," and methods he can use to light up his playing board in the game of kings.

As each new area is "lit up" with a flow of some kind of current, it shows new pathways and greater areas that can be "fed." In much the same way as his actions and influence build the "forest" around him as we mentioned in BERKANO, LAGUZ is a similar kind of concept that relies on currencies, both literal and figurative.

All kingship and rulership comes from these various kinds of currency, and a ruler without currency is no ruler at all.

The Inner Circle

INGWAZ is the enclosure around all the king has built. His castle walls are made up of shrewdness and silence, and the knowledge that there is always an inner circle, outside of which is the rest of the world. Ingwaz is both the council he holds close, and the company he keeps—a man is judged by his friends.

It is also the knowledge of when to hold and when to spend, when to plant, and when to reap. Timing is everything in the great game, and the ruler who cannot see when his cards should be played will be played himself.

INGWAZ is also the internal energy source upon which a king must draw, and feed, and draw from again. Without being able to feed himself an energy source of his own, he will lose heart, his strength will ebb, and he will "burn out" or "fade away." The best rulers are those who do not suffer from flagging or exhaustion because they have discovered a way to keep their energy contained, not sending it out needlessly in all directions.

OTHALA is the empire a ruler has built. This can be a country or corporation, a tribe, gang, body of work, or otherwise—but it is what will survive him after he is gone, or what he will bestow on his successor.

OTHALA is what the entire game is played for, the sum total of all the various parts the king has worked on—his forest of power, his sphere of influence, his creations, his followers, all his various currencies, coming together into a coherent whole that is his kingdom.

Strong rulers leave behind a legacy. Weak ones leave behind a carcass for the crows to pick at.

DAGAZ is time, the changing of eras, the hourglass against which we are all competing to accomplish what we can with the time we have. The normal human gives little thought to time beyond a vague dread of death and dissolution, but only because he has a basic fear of no longer being.

The man of power sees time and death as his ultimate competitor, and is motivated by them, spurred onward to play as many rounds of this game as he can before the timer runs out and he must pass his turn on to another.

This need to accomplish is almost unexplainable to those who do not feel its electrifying touch at the base of their spine—every morning, every moment.

DAGAZ is drive. The eternal moving force to succeed, the will to power that every ruler is born with.

The hard truth is that most leaders are born AND made.

Some were born to serve, and others to rule—those born without the light of DAGAZ coursing through them will be content to live lives of quiet satisfaction or desperation down in the fields.

Those who were birthed under its mark know that it is a crown that shines like the sun, but evades most hands that reach for it.

It is, like all the runes, many things at once, and as such, it is also a Doorway. It is a doorway that leads those intrepid enough to enter through it to legend. To glory, and to lasting fame—the only kinds of immortality that exist.

✣How to Start a Gang: a Blueprint✣

The questions I am asked the most almost invariably have to do with the "how to's" of gang building. I say gang, not tribe, because this word "tribe" has been beaten to death in recent years, and almost always used either incorrectly or as a marketing term.

Gang, on the other hand, derives from the Old Norse *gang*, and carries a much simpler meaning, "passage, way." Although laden with ill-meaning in our current society and carrying criminal connotations, a gang is simply a group of people going a certain way together.

Its definition in Old Norse is also something of an esoteric way of looking at it, in that a gang can certainly be a passage or doorway out of one way of living, and into another. For me, it has provided an escape from the way of life that the Empire would have chosen for me, and given me an alternative to the vapid, the temporary, and the friendships and confederations of convenience so often seen in the modern world.

Most guys want to know how to start a gang, but perhaps they would be better served by asking the question "should I?" Everyone wants to think of themselves as a leader, but this is not often the case. Refer to some of the leadership principles in this issue and decide whether you have what it takes—if you're not ready, look to join an established group that you can mesh with.

I have said time and time again that it is better to be an excellent lieutenant than a terrible leader. Often times, men's ego can't handle being second in command, or part of the body of the organization. They can't stand not being seen as "the main man." This is a character flaw and a weakness that should be rooted out.

Not everyone is either capable or ready to lead, and the ability to see this is often the difference between someone who could be a solid leader someday and someone who will never see the path to leadership because of their own hang-ups.

+Basic Tenets+

If you decide to start a gang, the first thing to settle are its basic tenets. What is it founded around? This can be as simple as a block of territory or as complex as a religious belief, but at the end of the day, it is the entire reason for your existence once you get things moving.

Because here at the beginning, I will tell you—a gang becomes your life, or it isn't a gang. As it develops, and grows, the framework of your day will be built around it, your night life, your work, your free time—all of it will center around the gang.

If you are looking for a hobby, look somewhere else. Doing this requires a full time commitment. The tenets of the gang will contribute to its entire texture and feel. The things you care about as a group will find their way into your tattoos, artwork and music. They will dictate the things you do together as a gang, and what your gang looks like and so on.

If your group is centered around cars or motorcycles, it will likely center around working on and riding or driving vehicles. Because of this, most gang activity will happen on the road, at parties, in the garage, and so on. Depending on the nature of the group, the bikes might all have a specific "look" in order to hard signal belonging to your gang and its values.

If your gang centers around the Orthodox Christian faith, its events are likely to be spiritual in nature. Iconography and meeting places are a no-brainer here.

At the end of the day, what you decide upon as your basic, bedrock tenets will determine the future of the gang, so know what it is you want to be about, and be about it—make everything about it, from the way you look to the car you drive to the way you approach life.

+Confederation+

Next, you will have to determine how you will confederate. What separates "you" from "them?" In the Wolves, we confederate under a very specific oath that we swear when we become "full members," and the words of this oath are what we base our group's behavior on.

There must be something that marks the boundary between "in" and "out" and this can look like anything you want it to. It's your gang, but remember that human beings respond to ritual. There should be a transition for your prospective members that leads them from the outside to the inside, possibly as a long process, but maybe not.

You might decide that once someone wants in, and adheres to the tenets of the group, they are just "in," but it is my recommendation that you do something slightly more "heavy" than this. I've seen guys "jumped in" to groups, I've witnessed new Christians get baptized, new members receive tattoos, performed rituals in the woods around roaring fires as new members spoke oaths of allegiance and servitude to the gang.

Whatever you do, make it interesting.

+Members+

Without members, there is no gang.

How will your gang attract new members?

How will someone become a member once they are interested?

These two questions pretty much encompass the whole idea of membership. The first is simply, how do you get members? The answer is, if your gang is "niche" enough, that is, not just some generic, worthless affiliation of normal people, it will attract people who identify with that niche.

In our current world, social media and the internet can be a great tool, but most gangs rely on locality in order to drive their activities—its sort of hard to "be a gang" when members live hours away from each other, so its recommended you look locally.

Flyer, go to events that make sense for your gang, hard signal your affiliation so people can see you are "part of something." This is the entire reason for motorcycle club jackets, bandanas, tattoos, club shirts and so on. If no one knows it exists, no one can join. That being said, secrecy can be a draw of its own, as long as the "right people" know about it.

Once you've attracted some potential members, what will the process be to bring them into the gang?

Bikers and many others use a "prospecting" phase, and most gangs use this same strategy in one form or another, where a guy who wants to join goes through a process of serving the gang and showing his intentions are correct. He might learn the gang's history, clean the clubhouse, do chores for members, or things might be more extreme.

He might be "on call" 24-7 while he is probationary, at the beck of all full members, or there might be events that are mandatory for him to attend.

Decide this stuff before you get started, because trust me, it is a lot more difficult to change things down the road than it is to think about it at the beginning.

+Activities+

What do you do as a gang? This will largely depend on your basic tenets as we discussed earlier, but gang activities make up the entire backbone of your experience as a group, so knowing the kind of things you will do together will dictate the texture of gang life for a member.

Maybe you will go to the gym together a certain amount of times a week, and hold monthly events. Perhaps you will travel a certain amount of miles on hiking trails, if your gang is centered around outdoor activities.

You might garden, or graffiti, or fight, or build something.

Probably, you will do a combination of the above, but a majority of a leader's job is to create a world in which your members exist, and this means having things to do.

Another important consideration is that gang activity, and the enjoyment and fulfilling nature thereof is what keeps current members and attracts new ones. You can't just perform chores together because people will get bored or disenfranchised.

Life together must be enjoyable for members, otherwise no one would ever join.

This seems like a no-brainer, but I have seen a hundred gangs come and go because some guy builds a group of guys that he can boss around. That's not how it works.

As a leader, you are a provider, and are responsible for gang life. Parts of it will be work, sure, but any group that bases itself around hardship only will see itself break apart rapidly.

There must be fulfillment and a family element that brings people together.

Don't make it harder than it has to be: dinner together, poker night, bar raids, camping, parties and so on are the elements of fun that make the hard work worthwhile. Again, your tenets will dictate what you do for fun as well—obviously a straight edge gang is not going to go to the bar for its "down time," but it has to have some sort of enjoyable activities if it is to attract and retain membership.

+Land+

You must purchase your own space.

There's not much to say about this really, but owning property or a building, from the simplest clubhouse or church to hundreds of acres—you can't rely on other people to provide you with your place to be yourselves.

This should be paramount on your list of goals as a group: own your space.

+Innovation/Growth+

Once you've gotten going, you can start to grow organically, to innovate and bring dynamics in as they are needed. A lot of people think themselves to death before getting something started, but I always recommend you keep it simple.

Decide on your tenets, your membership rules, and gang activities fast and loose. Have a solid sketch that you can build the meat and muscle onto as you go, otherwise you'll be like a commander who is stuck deciding on the embroidery for uniforms on an army that doesn't exist.

Innovation is crucial to the continuation of a gang of men. It keeps things fresh and interesting, keeps the challenges coming and staves off boredom and stagnation.

Always be thinking of how you can improve, how you can tighten things up, keep it enjoyable, deepen members experience, thicken the bonds of loyalty to each other, and elevate members to better versions of themselves as they exist within the gang.

Find members specific jobs as the need arises. People who have a specific task or role in a group feel more important and more fulfilled, but never create jobs just to do it. Make sure everything you do fills a need, rather than creates rules or red tape for its own sake.

There is a perfect line somewhere between just enough rules and too many—experiment to find this. No one joined a group to have every second of their lives dictated—a good gang inspires its members to give their all, without having to demand it.

Always examine yourself as leader. Are you doing enough? Are you working harder than the members? Are you providing the group with direction, action, and a future?

At the end of the day, life in a gang of men is the most fulfilling thing I have ever done, the most frustrating, the most rewarding, the most valuable.

When in doubt, do like my friend Jack says —

Start the World.

Made in the USA
Monee, IL
19 July 2020